FRIENDSHIP TROUBLES

dealing with fights, being left out, and the whole popularity thing

by Patti Kelley Criswell

illustrated by Angela Martini

★ American Girl®

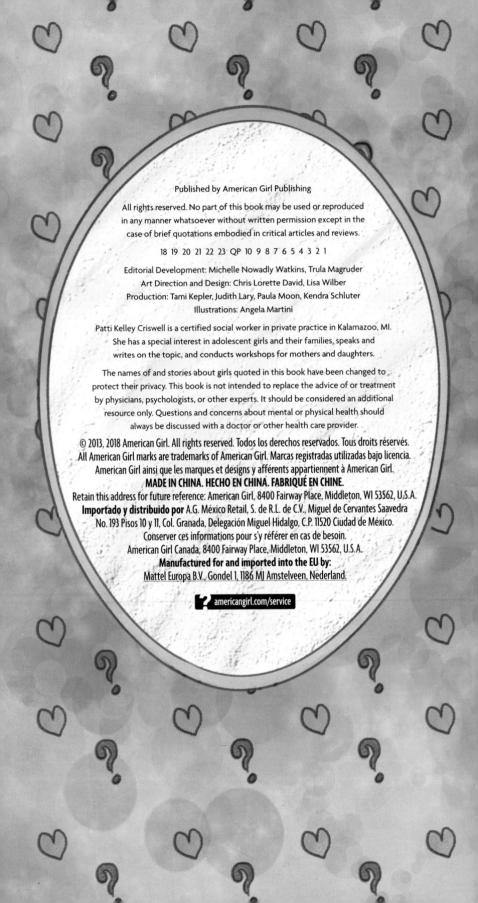

Published by American Girl Publishing

18 19 20 21 22 23 QP 10 9 8 7 6 5 4 3 2 1

Editorial Development: Michelle Nowadly Watkins, Trula Magruder
Art Direction and Design: Chris Lorette David, Lisa Wilber
Production: Tami Kepler, Judith Lary, Paula Moon, Kendra Schluter
Illustrations: Angela Martini

Patti Kelley Criswell is a certified social worker in private practice in Kalamazoo, MI.
She has a special interest in adolescent girls and their families, speaks and
writes on the topic, and conducts workshops for mothers and daughters.

The names of and stories about girls quoted in this book have been changed to
protect their privacy. This book is not intended to replace the advice of or treatment
by physicians, psychologists, or other experts. It should be considered an additional
resource only. Questions and concerns about mental or physical health should
always be discussed with a doctor or other health care provider.

americangirl.com/service

Dear Reader,

Thousands of girls have sent us letters about their friends. We've read how great it is to have a good friend and to be one, too. Many letters, though, are about friendship troubles, and girls ask: What do I do when friendship hurts?

In this book we've tried to answer your questions. Inside you'll find advice for solving your friendship problems. Tips and quizzes will help you get to know your friends—and yourself—a little bit better. Plus, you'll meet girls who've gone through serious friendship troubles and learn how they survived.

Every girl has what it takes to be a great friend and to choose friends who are right for her. We hope this book helps you do just that.

Your friends at American Girl

contents

all about friends

Remember kindergarten? Back then, friendships were pretty easy. Your parents arranged your play dates. If you and your friend had a fight about who got the cherry lollipop, an adult stepped in and calmed things down.

Now you're older, and a lot's changed. You're choosing your own friends and trying to solve your own problems. You need more from your friends, and they need more from you.

You've learned that a true friendship is a two-way street, and that both people have to work to make a relationship a success. You listen to your friend when she's having a bad day, and she does the same for you. Neither one of you is "in charge." You're equal. You can compromise when you need to, and you both know that your opinions matter.

Every friendship is a little different. You may value one girl for the way she makes you laugh when you're down. You may value another for the way she helps you solve problems. Underneath it all, though, the best friendships share some very basic things.

what makes a great friend?

What some girls say:

"A really good friend has to be able to understand you and the way you think, appreciate you for who you are, and always keep your secrets. When a friend lies, it can ruin a friendship for a long time."

"A real friend sticks up for you in tough situations."

"A friend should be someone you are comfortable with—not someone who you are afraid will laugh at you."

"I like a friend who is nice, truthful, and fun to be with. Also creative, so we are never bored."

"A true friend doesn't get mad at every little thing."

"I think a real friend is someone who likes you for who you are. My best friend is more popular than I am and has a lot more friends than I do. She has so many other choices, but she picked me because she likes me."

"Someone who will encourage me."

"A friend is dependable and doesn't just say she will be there and not show up. It's a trust thing."

What you say

Think about it. What do you think makes a great friend? On a piece of paper, make a list of qualities that a girl should have to be one of your good friends. Put a ☆ next to the things you can't do without.

true friend test

Good friends are good for you. How do your buddies measure up? Picture each girl in your mind and ask yourself whether these statements are true or not.

After we're together, I feel happy and
good about myself.

yes   no

When something good happens, she's the first one
I want to tell, because I know she'll be really
excited for me.

yes   no

When I'm angry about something and just need
to talk, she'll listen.

yes   no

When I say, "OK, we'll do it your way,"
it doesn't feel like I'm giving in, because chances are that
the last time we disagreed, she did things my way.

yes   no

She brings out the best in me.

yes   no

We never run out of things to talk about.

yes   no

When she's sad or upset, I feel bad and want to
help in any way I can.

yes   no

I can make a total fool of myself, and she won't cut me down for it.

yes   no

I would stand up for her, and I know she'd do the same for me.

yes   no

We can sit and work on a project or watch TV and not say a word—it never feels awkward.

yes   no

answer:

The girl who inspires you to say yes to these statements is a friend through and through. **Hold on to her.**

And the others? Well, it's the rare friendship that's absolutely perfect. But answering no many times is not a good sign. Just because you've been friends with a girl for a long time or because you spend a lot of time together doesn't mean a friendship is true-blue.

Friendship File
Lydia

Lydia is short, spunky, and creative. She used to hang out with four or five other girls at school, and while she wasn't the most popular girl, she wasn't at the bottom of the heap, either. Lydia loved to speak her mind (which sometimes got her into trouble), but she also loved to help people. She figured her friends felt the same way, so when tragedy struck, she turned to them.

What happened

Lydia's brother, Randy, injured his spine diving into shallow water at a lake. He lost the use of his legs and had to learn to use a wheelchair. Randy was two years older, and a big brother Lydia loved and admired. His accident hit her hard—really hard.

Lydia felt so sad and scared that she hardly knew what to do. Sometimes she shared these feelings with her parents, but she knew that they were hurting, too. She didn't want to add to their worries. So she carried her grief to school and talked with her friends. Sometimes they listened, but they didn't say much. Lydia could see that her friends felt awkward. It was like they just didn't get it. After a while, she stopped talking about her brother and pretended that everything was fine.

But it wasn't fine. Lydia needed to feel close to someone. She got clingy. She would try to be involved in every conversation that took place, be a part of everything that was going on. She remembers, "I was totally hyper—I was terrified of being left out!" But that's just what happened. Annoyed by Lydia's neediness, the other girls kicked her out of the group. They even wrote a long list of "annoying things about Lydia" and gave it to her. So just when she thought the situation couldn't get any worse, it did.

What she did

Lydia was heartbroken. She spent more time at home, holding tight to her family. She cried a lot. When she became, as she says, "mad as all get-out," she'd write songs and play them on the piano or the violin. Music really helped.

After a few weeks, Lydia struck up a conversation with a girl named Grace. Grace sat in the back of the classroom and kept mostly to herself. Lydia had hardly noticed her before. Now the two hit it off and started to hang out together. Before long they were inseparable. Lydia remembers, "Grace never got tired of me." Lydia joked that Grace was an "angel" sent to help. And Grace did help. She stuck it out with Lydia during that whole awful time. When Lydia ranted and raved about people who weren't handicapped and who parked in the handicapped spots, Grace listened. And when Lydia could do nothing but cry as she watched her brother struggle, Grace was there. One day when Grace knew Lydia was feeling really down, she showed up with two pink roses, just to say she cared.

How it worked out

As Lydia's family adjusted and accepted their new challenges, Lydia's life grew more stable. Today, Grace remains one of Lydia's best friends. The old group? Well, they eventually started being nice to Lydia again. She gets along with them, but it will never be the same. She looks back now and says, "They're not bad people. They just had no idea what the true meaning of friendship is, and I guess I didn't, either." But she does now. She absolutely does.

respect

You've heard the word your whole life—at home, in school, everywhere: respect. "Respect adults," "Respect yourself," "Respect the rules," "Be respectful," and so on.

So what does respect have to do with friendship? Everything.

Respect

Respect is what you offer a friend because you honor the friendship.

Friendship

You could treat a friend rudely—nobody's going to give you detention or ground you if you do. But you choose not to do that. You want your friend to know how much she means to you. Of all the things that can bind two people together, respect may be the strongest.

Having respect for someone else means

- resisting the temptation to talk about your friend behind her back, even when you're angry.
- trusting that her intentions are good ones.
- believing her when she says she's sorry.
- being happy for her even when you're really jealous.

Showing a friend respect takes effort—but it's worth it. With trust and respect, you and your friend will have fewer problems, solve them more easily, and enjoy each other a whole lot more.

The thing I look for most in friends is how open-minded they are. I think it's important that my friends can respect me for who I am.

friendship hot spots

So you've found a great friend. She has all the qualities you value most, and in so many ways she's perfect. That's it. **Right?**

Uh-uh. It's not that easy. Friendships need care every bit as much as that flower in the garden needs water. Even the best of friends have problems now and again. Maybe your feelings are hurt because your friend walked home with someone else when you expected her to walk with you. Maybe you're annoyed because she calls ten times a night. Maybe you're jealous of her big success, or she's jealous of yours. It isn't as if your friendship is in doubt, really, but things aren't so wonderful, either.

You've hit a friendship hot spot. It's probably not a big deal: a lot of trouble comes from mistakes and miscommunication. But even a little problem can rub and rub like a stone in your shoe until it makes a real sore. **The time to deal with it is now.**

best friends?

A best friend can be as comforting as a cup of hot cocoa on a cold winter's night. She listens, she keeps your secrets, and when you're together, it just feels right. You feel safe and secure knowing she's there when you need her.

But there may be times when having a best friend makes you feel tied down. Do you always need to sit with her at the movies? Can you never be partners with someone new? What if you want to be close with another girl, too? Is that OK? What if your best friend feels angry or jealous? What do you do?

Are best friends a good idea or a bad one?

It depends. For some girls, having a best friend feels like too much pressure. For others, it's the only way to go. If that's you, here are two things to remember.

One: Don't get into a tight relationship with just anybody. If you can't be yourself with a girl, then proclaiming yourselves "best friends" isn't a good idea. It's better to let your friendship grow for a while. If you want to get closer, work on the little conflicts that come along. Let her know what you enjoy about her friendship and what you would like to see change.

Two: Even best friends aren't best friends every single day. Friendships are like a dance. You get close for a while, then you pull away, and then you get close again. That's normal. Keep talking to your friend when you're feeling more distant, but be sure you have other friends, too. Never put all your energy into a single friendship. That way, if you and your best friend aren't doing well this week, you aren't left out in the cold. In the end, that means a lot less pressure on the friendship.

I like having a group of good friends who all get along. That way, no one is singled out as being better than the others.

I do have a best friend. I don't tell my other friends, though, since I don't want them to feel left out.

I think it's OK to have a best friend as long as you have other friends, too.

left out

Just when you've found a friend you love spending time with, some other girl comes along and—**wham!** Those two start hanging out all the time, laughing at things you don't think are funny and leaving you feeling sick inside.

You're left out, rejected, abandoned. It's one of the world's lousiest feelings, but you're not alone. **Most girls feel left out at one time or another.** Your first impulse may be to blame the third girl in the triangle. Don't. Nobody ever wins the blame game—honestly. It always does more harm than good. You may also feel like marching over to your friend's house and saying, "OK, pick. It's her or me!" But what if she doesn't choose you? Anyway, YUCK. Is this what friendship is really about?

Instead, talk to your friend. Let her know that you are feeling left out. She may be able to reassure you with words or by spending more time with you.

You should also ask yourself whether your friend is really shutting you out or simply enjoying a new relationship. There's no official limit on how many friends a girl can have. Why act as if there were? There must be a good reason your friend likes the new girl. Try to find out what it is. Give her a chance. Maybe you can be friends with her, too. Remember that as you grow and change, so will your friendships.

Of course, if your friend is truly ditching you, say, for the "popular" crowd, that's a different story. Try to **play it cool.** For now, spend time with your other friends. Tell yourself that your relationship with your good friend is changing—not ending, just changing. Her interest in the new group may fade as she gets to know those girls better. She may end up missing you and come back.

If she doesn't, you're going to hurt for a while—and sorely. But that time will pass, and you can come out of this with your head high, knowing that you were true to your friendship even if she wasn't.

Prescription for "being-left-out-itis"

Your friend doesn't call and doesn't call. You feel pooped, the world looks gray, and you've been trying to persuade your parents to move to Tahiti. Sound familiar? You've got a bad case of being-left-out-itis, and you need to do something before it gets worse. Doing something relaxing or productive or just plain fun will take the edge off your bad feelings. Try this:

Take one hot bath with sweet-smelling stuff and put on favorite pajamas. Apply blanket, pillow, and really good book. Let settle.

If symptoms persist, place head on shoulder of special person, wrap arms around person's chest, and squeeze.

Not your style?

Watch a movie and make popcorn.

Rearrange your room.

Sort through old photos.

Design your dream house.

Imagine where you will be in 5, 10, or even 20 years. Write it all down and put it away for safekeeping.

Most of all: Remember that the feelings you have now are temporary. Even if (IF) this friendship is truly over, you aren't going to be without friends forever. You're in between friends. Making a call to another girl is step one to getting your life back on track.

Friendship File

Jasmine

Jasmine always felt like an outcast. Her family was . . . well, a little different from other families. They grew their own food, made their own clothes, and didn't own a TV. Jasmine's parents also had LOTS of rules about what she could and couldn't eat: no soda, no candy, and no junk food. As a result, Jasmine had a hard time fitting in. She was thankful when she met Ellen, an open-minded girl who didn't make a fuss about Jasmine's family. Jasmine finally had the best friend she'd always wanted. Then along came Alex.

What happened

Alex moved to the neighborhood from New York City. Ellen was assigned to be her bus buddy and help her learn her way around the school. Alex was loud and funky and wore amazingly cool clothes. When Ellen and Jasmine got together, all Ellen could talk about was Alex. Before long, Jasmine found herself hating Alex. Alex was everything she wasn't. Jasmine felt sure she was losing Ellen as a friend. How could she compete when Alex had every color of glittery makeup possible, and she herself wasn't even allowed to use lip balm?

What she did

One day, Jasmine said sarcastically to Ellen, "Why don't you go be with your new best friend?"

Ellen asked, "What's going on? Why don't you like her?"

Jasmine started to say, "Because she eats the wrong kind of food, wears the wrong kind of clothes, and uses the wrong kind—" but she stopped herself. How could SHE, who had been picked on for being different, hate someone for that very reason? She was ashamed of herself. She pulled it together, apologized, and promised Ellen that she would try harder to get along.

How it worked out

In the beginning, it didn't. Jasmine still felt left out a lot. Ellen and Alex had inside jokes. "Guess you had to be there," they'd say. Deep down Jasmine knew Ellen cared about her—but it hurt! Out of fear and desperation, she decided to talk to Ellen and Alex again about how she was feeling.

Both Ellen and Alex apologized and promised "no more inside jokes." Jasmine and Alex agreed to wipe the slate clean and start over.

Jasmine also decided to talk to her mom and dad. Her parents had no idea what had been going on, and they wanted to help. They suggested that Jasmine spend more time with her writing and her music, which she loved. They also thought she should make an effort to do things with other friends. Jasmine agreed. She had depended on Ellen too much, and she resolved to reach out more to other girls.

In the end, Jasmine learned to appreciate Alex's style, and the three became good friends. Jasmine didn't lose Ellen's friendship, but she did have to share it. In return, she gained a friend in Alex and learned a lot about herself.

jealousy

Picture this: You spend breakfast arguing with your mom about whether or not Ms. Curdle, the world's most boring babysitter, is going to be your companion during spring break while your parents are at work. Then you wait, in the rain, for the bus. Just as you sit down, your friend Maddie bursts in, talking a mile a minute, with the news that her family is going to an amazing amusement park over spring break.

What do you do? What do you say? You're so jealous that you're seeing spots before your eyes. This is terrible! She's your friend. You're **NOT** supposed to feel this way, right?

Well, not quite. Let's face it, at one time or another, we all get bitten by the jealousy bug. We compare what we've got with what somebody else has and start grinding our teeth. It's normal, but it can also cause big-time trouble between friends.

Jealousy is poison.

You may want your friend's things. You may want her talents. Either way, you have to deal with the feelings before they rot the relationship.

Just admitting that you're jealous can help. Saying "I'm happy for you, but I'm really jealous, too" or "You're so lucky" helps your friend to know how you're feeling.

If your friend doesn't get it—if she's making things worse by bragging —give her a hint: "You seem really proud of your_____." Then change the subject. After a while she'll get the message.

You also need to remind yourself of some things that you already know. For one thing, there will always be kids who have way more than you do—just as there will always be kids who have way less. If you need to outdo everybody all the time, you'll never sleep. There'll be no end to it. Don't confuse what you want with what you need. Step back. How important is it, really, that a friend has a jacket that's cooler than yours? Yeah, you're jealous, but big deal. It's a jacket.

Finally, every girl has different strengths and weaknesses. Your friend may get to take a great trip, but she may also have problems that you're very glad aren't yours. Look at your own life. What do you love that you wouldn't trade for anything? What helps you to feel proud or grateful? Make a top-ten list. Hang it in your room, and read it now and then so that you don't forget.

P.S. If you're lucky enough to be the one going to an awesome amusement park?
Watch yourself. It's one thing to share your experiences and express yourself. It's quite another to brag. Be sensitive.

tough stuff

I have a friend who always wants me to help her by giving her all the answers. I want to tell her no, but I'm afraid she'll be hurt or she won't be my friend anymore! It's getting harder to do my own work now. Should I risk my friendship or my grade?
Answered Out

If the only way to keep this friendship is to cheat, it's not much of a friendship. Tell your friend that you're uncomfortable giving her the answers. If she dumps you, you'll know that she was using you. If she doesn't, you can offer her some real help. She's never going to get anywhere using other people's answers. But if you study with her, maybe she can get caught up.

I have a friend who copies every single thing I do. It's getting annoying. What should I do?
Bugged All the Time

When you express yourself—whether it's in how you dress or what you write—it makes you feel special and unique. When this friend copies you, it may feel like she's trying to take those feelings away. But she's not. Your friend admires you and your style and probably wants to see if it's a fit for her. She's paying you a compliment. Instead of getting angry, encourage her to come up with her own unique style by letting her know what you think is special about her. Remember, just because you did something first doesn't mean it's exclusively yours. It just means that you're a trendsetter!

I have this one weird friend. She eats off my plate and acts like I am her friend. I really don't want to hang out with her, but I don't know how to tell her without hurting her feelings.
Annoyed

Start by being honest. Tell her that when she eats off your plate, it grosses you out. Sometimes when people know what's bugging you, they can stop being so annoying. Of course, sometimes they can't. If that's the case here, and you truly don't want to be her friend at all, you need to break it off as gently as you can. Don't talk about her to other friends. It's cruel to get the whole school involved. Talk to her alone—without other people around. Tell her that you're feeling pressured by this friendship. You want to spend time with other girls for a while and hope that she can do the same. Be friendly, but keep your distance.

One of my friends gave me a "best friends" necklace. But I don't feel like she's my best friend. I don't want to hurt her feelings, but I don't want to give in, either. What should I do?
Unsure

You've taken the necklace. If you don't wear it, she may take the hint. She may also ask you about it. If she does ask, be honest. Say that you like her and are very flattered that she likes you, but that you don't feel closer to her than you do to other girls. Offer to return the necklace. If she accepts, give it back with a nice note or a token of your friendship attached.

working it out

There are problems in every close relationship. Every one.
It's a normal part of being friends.

Some problems are small. They start fast and end that way, too. Like
sprinkles of rain in your otherwise sunny friendship, they're no big deal.
But other problems feel like big whopping thunderstorms, complete with
lightning and fierce winds. They make you think your friendship could be in

total,

complete

CRISIS!

Did you know that the Chinese word for *crisis* also contains the symbol
for *opportunity*?

In every friendship problem, there IS an opportunity, as well as a choice.
You can end the friendship or work it out (and maybe even end up closer
than ever). Either way, you've got a job ahead of you.

do you speak up?

Even when you know what the problem is, it can be hard to face. How would you respond? Choose your answers.

1. A friend thinks she's being funny, but her comments about your new coat really tick you off. You . . .

   a. don't do anything.

   b. tell her that if she doesn't knock it off, she'll be sorry.

   c. think of something you can say to embarrass her and get her back.

   d. tell her you're upset and ask her to stop teasing you.

2. You just got new headphones for your MP3 player. On the way to school, your friend yanks them off and breaks them. You . . .

   a. pick them up and put them in your backpack, saying nothing.

   b. are furious and demand they be replaced by Friday.

   c. say nothing but tell everyone about what happened, making her look really bad.

   d. tell your friend that you're bummed. If she offers to replace your headphones, you let her. If she apologizes, you accept her apology. Otherwise, you chalk it up to experience—and leave your player and headphones at home.

3. A friend tells you that her mother has cancer. You tell someone else, and it gets around school. Your friend is unbelievably angry with you. You . . .

   a. avoid her at all costs.

   b. get angry back. It's not as if what you said wasn't true.

   c. blame the rumors on someone else.

   d. admit that you were very wrong. Apologize, and ask her what you can do to make things right.

4. You're at your friend's house when your friend starts being really disrespectful to her parents. You feel uncomfortable and decide to leave. Later, you . . .

a. apologize and beg for forgiveness.

b. blame your friend for having such a freaky family.

c. run home and e-mail everyone about the fight.

d. tell your friend how you felt, but reassure her that you're still her friend.

5. You know that your friend is mad at you. You've seen the signs. But she's not saying why, and you have zero idea what you've done. You . . .

a. say nothing and hope the situation gets better on its own.

b. get angry, too. Two can play this game!

c. share your troubles with other friends, saying, "I don't know why she's doing this to me!"

d. write her a note saying that you've noticed she's been giving you the cold shoulder. Tell her that you value the friendship and want to work things out.

how did you score?

mostly a's
You tend to push strong feelings away to avoid a conflict, even if it means you get hurt or taken advantage of. Problem is, your silence forms a wall between you and other people. Learn to share your feelings. Start by writing in a journal. Next, speak out more at home, and then with other people with whom you feel safe. It will be hard at first, but it's worth it.

mostly b's
Anger without self-control is like a car without brakes. Ask yourself, *Is it easy to be friends with me?* If you're always losing your cool, people will avoid you to keep from becoming targets. Give yourself time to calm down, and think before you react.

mostly c's
You're trying to get your message across, but you're going about it the wrong way. Getting other friends involved in your fights almost always makes things worse. Talk only to the person you're fighting with. Sharing your feelings may bring the two of you closer together.

mostly d's
You understand the value of communication in friendships. You're learning to be honest and sensitive to your friends' feelings —and to your own. Way to go!

the big picture

Q: How do you turn a little problem into a big one?

   a. By stewing about it and getting madder

   b. By not talking about it

   c. By blowing up

   d. All of the above   *right answer!*

Big important point:

It's absolutely OK to feel angry.

Anger is a natural response in some situations, and stuffing away your anger will only make you resentful. You need to talk about what's bothering you. But how you go about doing that is important. If you talk (or yell) before you think, you might say things you don't mean and can't take back. You'll become frustrated and make the situation worse.

So don't try to talk when you're really upset. Do whatever it takes to cool down and think things through. Walk away and go home, or say, "I have to go now. We can talk later," and hang up the phone.

Then:

Play with your dog.

Take a shower.

Listen to your favorite song.

Watch some cartoons.

Do whatever it takes to clear your head.

Now, look at the big picture. Why are you so mad? Are you hurt? Embarrassed? Is this about power? Is your friend trying to control you? Are you trying to control her? Decide what this problem is about—at least from your point of view.

If what you're upset about grew out of a specific incident, write down what happened or describe it to a grown-up. This will help you understand what happened and what part you played in it.

And **be honest.** You can be right about some things and wrong about others. Were you doing something your friend finds annoying? Not thinking about how she felt? Do you need to apologize?

For that matter, is what you are mad about worth it? Sometimes you may react to something and realize later that it wasn't really a big deal. Could that be happening here?

Other helpful questions:

Did my friend actually mean to do me harm? That is, is she really rotten, or did she just make a mistake?

Is this the first time that this has happened, or is it becoming a pattern?

Will I still be mad about this tomorrow? Next week?

What needs to happen for me to feel better?

Is what happened going to change my life? How?

Now decide: Is this worth fighting about?

❏ **Yes**   ❏ **No**

decision time

There are some things that friends just don't do to friends. These are the things you should not just "let go." If someone does them to you, you have to speak up.

Ask yourself these questions:

Did she threaten to hurt me physically?

Did she use me by taking advantage of my time or my kindness?

Has she been telling lies about me?

Did she care more about my stuff than about me?

Did she make me look stupid or humiliate me in front of a group of people or online?

Did she do things to hurt me on purpose?

Did she say rotten things about my family?

Did she try to force me to do things online I didn't want to do?

These are biggies. They are not OK and never will be.

Say something.
Speak up.
Talk to her.

Now you might be thinking:

But I can't confront her.

She'll get madder.

It's too hard.

I don't want to hurt her feelings!

You aren't the only girl who doesn't want to make waves. But you can do this. More importantly, you have to. Otherwise, the anger, hurt, and disappointment may shake around inside you until one day, a little crack will open up and—pow!—you explode like a bottle of soda that's been rolling around in the car. Or you may end up being a girl who continues to get pushed around by others.

Let your feelings out. Let people know that you're frustrated.

Big important point: If you can learn to take care of yourself—to stick up for yourself in relationships—you'll have learned one of life's most important lessons. Nobody can stomp on you unless you let them.

Nobody.

talk it out

Even though you're going to talk about what's happened and how you feel, you're not going to back your friend up against a wall—at least not if you want to resolve things. This talk doesn't have to be a fight, even if your emotions (and hers) are feeling pretty intense. It's all in your approach.

Can we talk?

Says "I want to resolve things."

Remember the other day? Well, it's been bothering me. I was really hurt by . . .

Being specific gives you two a problem to solve together.

How do you see what happened?

Says that you know she has a point of view, and you're willing to hear it.

I don't get what you mean. Could you explain it to me?

Says "I'm trying to cut you some slack."

Maybe we have to agree to disagree on that.

Says "I respect your opinion and can compromise some—but I expect my opinions to be respected, too."

Our friendship means a lot to me, and I want to work this out.

Says "I'm willing to do my part if you're willing to do yours."

more talking tips

Pick a good time and place to talk. You need privacy and a good chunk of time to get anywhere in this conversation. Soccer practice is not going to cut it. Talking on the phone is OK, but face-to-face is better. Steer clear of writing messages online or when texting. Misunderstandings abound in e-mails and text messages, and once you put something in writing, there's no taking it back.

Plan what you'll say beforehand. You should be telling your friend about your feelings, not her shortcomings. Got that? Stick to how you feel about what happened, not what a rotten friend she's been. If you start attacking her with insults and accusations, she's going to have to defend herself.

What's your objective in this conversation? What needs to happen for things to get back to normal? Do you need an explanation? An apology? Tell your friend what you want to happen to make things right.

Do you have something to apologize for? Now's the time to do it.

Listen, listen, and listen. Open your mind, and hear what your friend has to say. She has feelings, too.

What if you don't walk away with good feelings? Well, you may not be the friends you were before, but you don't need to be enemies, either. Check out the **time to go?** section on pages 56–57 for some advice on how to say good-bye.

when you lose it

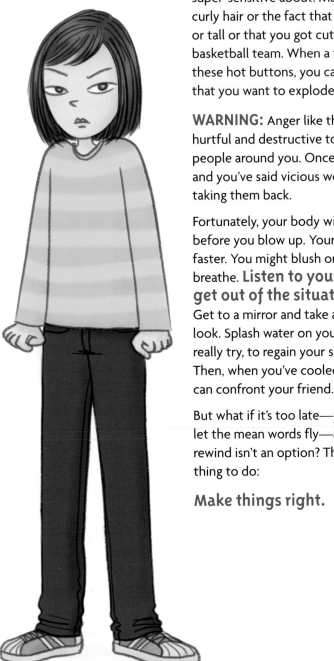

We all have certain things that we're super-sensitive about. Maybe it's your curly hair or the fact that you're short or tall or that you got cut from the basketball team. When a friend pushes these hot buttons, you can get so angry that you want to explode.

WARNING: Anger like this can be hurtful and destructive to you and the people around you. Once you've lost it and you've said vicious words, there's no taking them back.

Fortunately, your body will warn you before you blow up. Your heart will beat faster. You might blush or find it hard to breathe. **Listen to your body and get out of the situation—fast.** Get to a mirror and take a good, long look. Splash water on your face and try, really try, to regain your self-control. Then, when you've cooled down, you can confront your friend.

But what if it's too late—you've already let the mean words fly—and pressing rewind isn't an option? There's only one thing to do:

Make things right.

Here's how to make an apology:

- Be sincere and take responsibility for your actions. No blame, no excuses. Say the words: "I'm sorry."

- Be specific. Let your friend know how bad you feel for your part in the fight.

- Let her know what you wish you had done, and what you'll do next time.

- Reassure her that you value the friendship and will work hard not to let this happen again.

Here's how to receive an apology:

- Admitting you're wrong isn't easy for anybody. Hear your friend out. Listen HARD to what she is trying to say.

- Don't rehash the argument or bring up fights that happened in the past.

- Accept her apology. Accepting an apology doesn't necessarily mean you've forgiven her. It just means that you understand that she feels bad about what happened. (True forgiveness requires time to regain your trust in her as a friend.)

- Finally, consider whether you need to apologize for your part in the fight.

fight over?

I called my friends some really offensive names. I tried apologizing, but nothing worked. Is there a way I can make them forgive me?
Forgive Me Not

You can't make anybody do anything they don't want to do. All you can do is admit you were wrong and hope your friends remember that everybody makes mistakes. Give it time. Apologize again and be sure it's sincere. Let your friends know how angry you were. Tell them how you wish you'd handled the situation. Say that you'll never call them such names again. After that, it's up to them.
P.S. Remember that "sorry" doesn't always fix things. Decide now to get a better handle on your anger.

My friend and I got into a fight. We haven't talked all summer, and school is about to start. I am really scared to talk to her. What should I do?
Silent for Too Long

Call her. Sure, it will be awkward at first, but at least you'll find out where you stand. If you want to restore the friendship, try saying something like, "I'm really sorry for my part of what happened." This gives your friend the chance to say that she's sorry, too. If you just can't make the call? Write to her and tell her that you miss her and would like to start over. Do not use another friend as a go-between. Work this out yourself.

Here's what some girls say works for them:

"When we're mad, we go home, wait five minutes, and then call each other up and talk it out."

"When my friend and I get into a fight, we usually go for a walk and talk about it. Never give up. If you are friends, surely you can work it out!"

"We rate the problem from one to ten, with ten being really important and one being silly. Then we wait ten minutes and rate it again."

"The fight ends when someone says, 'This is stupid. Let's just respect each other's different opinions.'"

betrayal

When a girl says she's your friend, you believe her. You trust her to respect you and treat you well. You trust her with your feelings. You trust her with your secrets. That's why it's so awful when a friend betrays you. You feel

sad,

angry,

humiliated,

turned inside out,

and incredibly, incredibly confused.

"When my friend lied to me, I felt so hurt, I just wanted to crawl into a hole and never come out."

How could she ignore your feelings? How could someone who liked and accepted you turn on you so fast? Is this a one-time deal? If she wants you to take her back, should you do it? What if it happens again—and again? What are you willing to go through for this friendship?

When do you decide enough is enough?

the on-again, off-again friend

One day she lets you read her journal. The next day she acts as if you don't exist. She's not talking to you, so you have no idea why she's upset. How can you solve a problem when you don't know what it is?

Some dos and don'ts:

Don't try to get revenge by doing the same things she's doing to you. Anger can spread and make things much worse.

Don't fall apart. If you cry and beg her to tell you what's wrong, you'll look like a bucket of gelatin in July, and it will only make her feel more powerful. If she thinks she can control you, she'll try to do just that.

Don't, don't, don't blame yourself.

Do make it clear to her that you want to be her friend. Tell her calmly that you don't like what she's doing and that things will have to change for you to stay friends. (Turn back to the talk it out section on pages 36–37 for some ideas on how to make this conversation successful.)

Think this can't work in the real world? Read on.

Friendship File

Jenna

Jenna moved to a new school and met Cami. They instantly became best friends. They ate lunch together, passed notes, talked on the phone. For Jenna, it was heaven!

What happened

As Jenna began feeling more comfortable in school, she met some other girls. Suddenly, Cami changed. She gave Jenna evil looks in class, talked about her to other girls, and even jumped away when she saw Jenna in the hallway. Jenna didn't know what to do, so she didn't do anything. Within a few days, Cami was acting like her old self again.

But it happened again and again. And again and again, Jenna felt upset. Sometimes Cami would call Jenna to apologize, which only made Jenna more confused. Why was Cami doing this? Jenna could never seem to get an answer.

Jenna hated going to school because she never knew who would be there: Nice Cami or Mean Cami? Jenna became so knotted up inside that sometimes she would even throw up.

What she did

With her mom's help, Jenna came up with a plan. They called it
"Operation NO PUKE!" First, Jenna spent more time with other girls
and developed those friendships. Then, more importantly, Jenna decided
that her friendship with Cami had to change. Instead of forgiving Cami
(over and over) and going back to the same kind of friendship, Jenna
stopped thinking of Cami as her best friend—or even her next-to-best
friend. They could be friends, but not close ones.

Jenna let Cami know that if she started being mean again, their friendship
would end for good.

How it worked out

It was hard at first. The more Jenna pulled away, the nicer Cami got. It
was tempting for Jenna to make up with Cami, but talking with her mom
helped her remember the many times that Cami had hurt her feelings.
Plain and simple, Cami had run out of second chances to be Jenna's close
friend.

Cami and Jenna got along fine for the rest of the year. In fact, they even
worked on the same carnival committee at school. Best of all, Jenna's
worries went away—and stayed away—when she learned to stand up
for herself.

the loose-lipped friend

Trust is the glue that holds a friendship together. If you've got a friend who thinks it's more important to look cool than to keep your secrets, she's way off base. Is it possible to be friends with her? Sure. Close friends? Probably not, since you'll need to be careful about what you tell a girl who can't control her impulse to blab.

If you're tempted to tell your friend's secrets, remember this: Most people love to hear a juicy bit of gossip, but they don't necessarily respect the person who's spreading it. And they definitely don't trust her.

The Secret Test

How smart are you about secrets? Pick each statement that you think is true.

It's OK to tell a secret that someone told you . . .

1. if you make the person you tell swear not to tell anybody else.

2. if you don't like the person the secret is about.

3. if the secret is likely to get out anyway.

4. if you don't reveal who the secret is about and just say "he" or "she" instead.

5. if keeping the secret could put the person who told you— or someone else—in danger.

Answers: The only true statement is number 5. If the secret could endanger someone, tell an adult. Some girls think 1–4 are true, too, but they aren't. It may seem like sharing top-secret news will impress other girls, but it may cost you a friend—and get you a reputation as a blabbermouth.

My friend trusted me with a really big secret. It's about her parents' marriage! I want to tell someone, but she told me not to tell anyone. What do I do?
Confused

Do just what she asked you to do: Keep her secret. As overwhelming as this secret might be, you need to honor her request. If you have to talk about it, talk only with your mom or dad—and make sure they know your friend wanted to keep this private. Sharing this secret with the wrong person could cause trouble that would make a hurricane look tame. Think about that—and zip your lips.

I told my friends about a secret admirer letter that I got. They promised not to tell anyone, but they did tell—the whole class! This was over a year ago, but I'm afraid that I can't trust them anymore!
Not to Be Trusted?

Maybe it's time to give them another chance. It was more than a year ago, after all. Start with a small secret and see what happens.

the backstabber

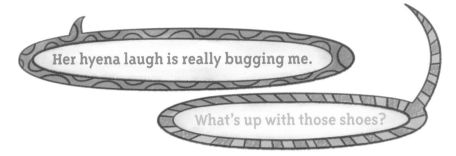

If you can't say something to a friend's face, then you shouldn't say it at all.

Good advice. Then why is it so hard to follow?

Truth is, at one time or another, most of us give in to the temptation to bring other people down. It makes us feel better than they are, more powerful. But that feeling is short-lived. Saying mean things about a friend behind her back is never a good decision. All it will do is lose you the trust of those around you.

Stop the backstabbing now!

Here's how:

- Assume that everything you say behind a person's back will get back to her.

- If talk turns mean, change the subject. Chances are people will do the same for you.

- Stop. Think about what you're going to say before you say it.

- Watch what you put in writing. Letters, notes, e-mails, and text messages have a way of sprouting wings and flying into the wrong hands.

And if you're the victim? Ouch. It hurts!

"I just found out my best friend has been saying really terrible things about me. I'm crushed!"

If this happens to you, first find out if it's true. **Go to your friend and talk to her.** Find a good time when you can talk one-on-one. But do it soon. Don't let it slide. Try not to involve others. It puts them in the middle and usually only confuses things.

And if your friend has been bad-mouthing you, find out what's behind it. Was your friend angry? Was there a misunderstanding? You need to find out what she was thinking and what she is willing to do to make things right again.

If you deserve an apology, ask for one.

No one deserves to be treated badly.
No one deserves to be treated badly.
No one deserves to be treated badly.

Say it again and again until you believe it.

are you in a toxic friendship?

Sometimes friends stop bringing out the best in each other. They betray their friendship in small ways and start to poison the relationship. Is your friendship toxic? Answer the questions to find out.

1. When you're together, do you spend most of your time competing with each other?

yes   no

2. Do you find yourself purposely doing things that bother her?

yes   no

3. Do you silently cheer when something bad happens to her?

yes   no

4. Do you feel bad about yourself after spending time with her?

yes   no

5. Do you feel obligated to spend time with her, even when you don't really feel like it?

yes   no

answers

If you answered **yes** to any of these questions, it's like a big red warning flag. Here's what you need to know:

1. If you two haven't had **an honest talk about competition,** have it now. Maybe you can make algebra grades and soccer skills (or whatever) off-limits and start over. If you two can't back off? It may be a friendship to phase out.

2. Doing things for spite may give you a moment's satisfaction, but it will cost you when the closeness you've felt for your friend fades away. Make a decision: **Are you this girl's friend or not?**

3. **Yuck.** You must have a whole lot of resentment stored up to feel like this. Ask yourself what this is really about. Is it something you can talk to her about? If so, try. If not, let the friend and these poisonous feelings go.

4. Do you think that your friend is feeling the same way? Maybe she is trying to bring you down to make herself feel better. Or maybe the two of you are deliberately bringing each other down. **Tell her how you feel.** If things don't change, you need to take a break from this friendship.

5. **Ease up.** Friends don't have to be chained at the leg. In fact, with a really good friend, you should never feel controlled. Be honest and tell her how you feel. If being honest makes things worse, though, you may need to step away from this friendship for a while.

time to go?

It's been a long time coming. You've thought about it—and cried about it—for months. Maybe you bring out the worst in each other. Maybe you're going in different directions. Whatever went wrong, this friendship just isn't working out. You want out—but how?

Some friendships just kind of fizzle. You stop putting out the effort, your friend does the same, and the relationship slowly fades away.

This is ideal. This girl makes a better friend than enemy. So allowing a friendship to fade gives you each a chance to walk away with your pride intact. If that's not possible and you feel a confrontation coming on, be gentle. **You don't want to rehash every fight you've ever had.** And you don't want to talk behind her back or be mean about it. Instead, just suggest taking a break. Instead of *ending* a friendship, think of it as *suspending* it for a while.

What **DO** you do? Start by telling your friend straight out:

We need to take a break for a while.

If she asks for a reason, be honest, but don't be hurtful. Let her know that you can still be friends—just not as close for now.

Be polite. Just because you're not a good match now doesn't mean it has to be awkward. Say hi in the halls, and be pleasant when you see her in gym class.

It's harder, obviously, if your friend is the one who wants to take a break and you want to hold on to the relationship. But either way, it's a big change.

This would be a good time to step back and look at your life and to make other changes, too. Talk with your parents. They have great shoulders for crying on, if you need that. If you're looking for new friends and new activities, they may have ideas that will help.

You'll also need to look at what you want in a friendship. Take some time to make a list. And look at your own friendship skills, too. Do they need brushing up? We all make mistakes. Try to learn from yours.

Finally, be good to yourself. It's not easy starting over, but somewhere out there is a girl just waiting to meet someone like you.

bullies & rule setters

What do you think of when you hear the word "bully"? The big thug who steals kids' lunch money? Or how about the boys on the bus who throw spitballs at the younger kids? True, those kids are bullies, but they're not the only kind of bullies running around.

Girls can be bullies, too. Their bullying may not be as obvious as that of the big meanie on the playground, but it's just as hurtful (maybe more hurtful). Some of these girls may even pass themselves off as friends.

Bullying isn't about friendship, though. It's not done in fun. It's mean-spirited and cruel, and it's meant to hurt. Whether a girl is making fun of your clothes or taking your gel pens, it's all about power. When you are the target of a bully, she's got more power and you've got less—way less.

Your power lies in the part of you that's in charge—the strong, smart part of you. If someone is trying to take your power, you're being bullied. And if you're being bullied, you have to fight back.

the whole popularity thing

There are two kinds of popular.

One girl seems to have it all together. She knows how to make others feel good about themselves. The way she carries herself just makes people want to be around her. People admire her, and that brings her popularity.

Then there's the popularity that's based on **POWER.** The girl who gets her popularity this way believes that if she can make others feel small, unimportant, and desperate, she'll come out on top. This girl isn't trusted or liked—she's feared. This type of girl is nothing more than a

bully.

Secret: **She's not going to be popular later in life because she won't have won the respect of friends—or the admiration of anyone.**

Emily Sophia Taylor
Grace Sarah Emma
Annie Olivia Eva Isabella Alyssa Clara
nnah Ashley Abigail Madise
Alex

Bullies come in all sorts of packages. Here are a few:

The Pretender

The pretender sweetly asks a girl a question, only to report back to her clique and humiliate the girl.

> Hey, Morgan, so what do you think of Jeffrey?

"He's nice."
Later: "Morgan has a crush on Jeffrey!"

The Intimidator

This girl uses threats to try to gain power.

> Do as I say, or you'll be sorry.

The Harrasser

Day in and day out, she targets certain kids and abuses them with cruel remarks.

> Hey, dork! Think you could look any dorkier today? No wonder you don't have any friends.

The Rule Setter

She sets "the rules" and decides who's in and who's out of her group.

> Check out what Sonya is wearing. I don't think so! She is so not sitting with us.

Friendship File
Brenna

Brenna was your average kid. She didn't get into trouble, didn't like to make waves, and generally sailed through life without too many problems. She had a few good friends and got along well with all the girls in her class—until LeeAnn came along. LeeAnn was popular and outspoken, and she liked telling others how it was going to be.

What happened

It all started at the school carnival. LeeAnn was there and she was a whiz at the ring-toss game. She kept playing and won stuffed animals for a few of her close, very popular friends. When LeeAnn was out of quarters, she sweetly asked Brenna if she wanted a stuffed animal and offered to win one for her. Brenna was suspicious but agreed. With Brenna's quarters, LeeAnn won the most adorable purple frog. Brenna took it, beaming.

Later, LeeAnn told Brenna that since she had played the game, Brenna had to give her the frog. Brenna looked around at the other girls holding their animals. "You said you'd win it for me, and after all, they were my quarters," Brenna said. LeeAnn didn't care. She kept after Brenna until a teacher noticed and took the frog. When the carnival ended, the teacher returned the frog to Brenna. But it didn't stop there. For days after, LeeAnn demanded the frog. She would act nice to Brenna and then suddenly turn on her. One day LeeAnn said that she wanted to trade the bear she had won for Brenna's frog, but she wouldn't show Brenna the bear. Turns out, it had been all chewed up by LeeAnn's dog! When Brenna didn't hand over the frog, LeeAnn became very mean. She threatened to make Brenna's life "worse than she could ever imagine."

What she did

That night Brenna went home and spilled the whole story at the dinner table. Her mom said, "Just give LeeAnn the frog, for goodness' sake!" and her grandmother agreed. But her two big brothers said, "No WAY! You give her the frog now, and what will be next?" Her dad said, "Just ignore her. She'll get tired eventually." Brenna went online that night and asked her cousin what she would do. Her cousin suggested Brenna change schools! Brenna was so confused. She wrote out all her options and thought about each one. Then she decided to stand up to LeeAnn once and for all.

How it worked out

The next day LeeAnn approached Brenna in the cafeteria. Brenna was shaking inside. She took a deep breath and said, "LeeAnn, I'm never going to give you the frog. It's not going to happen, and you need to stop asking me about it. If you continue to hassle me, I'm going to the counselor's office." LeeAnn called her a mean name and walked away.

LeeAnn continued to give Brenna dirty looks for about a week. Then LeeAnn finally gave up and left Brenna alone. Brenna felt really proud of herself. She and LeeAnn weren't friends (they never had been), but they weren't enemies, either. Brenna also knew that the next time someone tried to intimidate her, she would be ready. She could handle it.

You've heard it before. **"Just ignore her. She'll get tired of picking on you and find someone else."** And she might. It depends on how long you are willing to wait, and what you are willing to put up with in the meantime.

Here's what you should know:

- **Ignoring works best if it's used from the get-go.**
  The bully is trying to see if she can get you upset. Don't let her
  —or at least don't let her see you upset!

- **Look annoyed or bored with it all,** not scared and especially
  not hurt. Annoyed. Like she's just a bug that keeps flying around you.

- **Get a calendar.** Every day she hassles you, mark a big X by the date.
  Give it a few weeks. If things haven't started to fizzle out, you may
  need to take another approach.

- **Clue in the teacher.** Tell her what's happening and say you're
  choosing to ignore it for now. Your teacher may catch the bully
  in the act, and you won't even have to get involved.

Set limits.

We all have our limits. What are yours? Don't be anyone's doormat.
You've tried to get this girl to stop bothering you. If you've given her
fair warning and she's just not backing off, it's time to say

enough.

Involve the school. Be prepared to talk about what has been happening.
Recall specific words that the bully used and any threatening body
language. Most important, tell an adult about all the things that you
did to get this girl to stop bullying you.

Feel a little guilty? DON'T. You're not in the wrong here. The bully chose
to break the rules and threaten you. You chose not to take it.

Truth is, this girl is in for a tough life. Girls who bully others have trouble
solving problems—and this one is certainly going to find her fair share of
those. You're coming out of this better than she is. By handling the situation maturely, you've learned not only how to stand up for yourself but
how to go about it the right way—and that will take you much farther in
life than bullying ever could.

clever comebacks

Here's what other girls say about handling bullies:

I stay cool. I don't lose it. I just laugh and say "whatever" or try to say something funny. Then I forget about it.

If someone says something rude to me, I say, "Uh-huh, OK, yeah, right." Then I roll my eyes and walk away.

When this happens to me, I usually use sarcasm. "That's great!" or "I would care because . . . ?" are some of my responses.

I just pretend I didn't hear anything. Why should I let one person ruin my day?

I make a comeback, but not a rude one. I would say, "That wasn't very nice. How would you like it if I said that to you?"

I usually ignore it, but if the person says something extra-rude, I normally say something like "Really? I didn't know that!" or "Cool!"

If someone says something mean to me, I usually have something clever to say that isn't too harsh but gets across the point that I won't let people push me around —like "That's your opinion, but it's not mine!"

Usually if someone says something rude, I simply say, "If I valued your opinion, then I would be offended by that." It usually works to put her off guard.

I say "Thanks!" The girl usually looks at me like I am crazy, but I don't let her know that she hurt my feelings.

talking to your parents

P: "What's wrong?"

G: "Nothing."

Many girls are afraid or embarrassed to ask their parents for help. The last thing they want is for their parents to step in and try to "fix" the problem (and maybe make it worse). That's understandable, so why not tell the adults in your life what you really need? Here's an example of a conversation that can help:

P: What's wrong?

G: I've had a tough time at school lately. I could use someone just to listen.

P: What's going on?

G: I'm nervous about telling you, because I don't want you to freak out or lecture me. I need you to hear me out and then help me figure out the best way for ME to handle this.

P: I'm not so sure. If something is happening to you, I want to help!

G: You can help, but not by going to the school—at least not yet. I want to try to handle this my way first. If it doesn't work, then you can get involved. Deal?

P: Deal.

G: All right, here goes. Please just listen. No advice yet, OK? There's this girl . . .

. . . So now you know the whole story. What do you think I should do? Wait, let me get a pen. We'll write down our ideas.

P: You bet.

P: (Once the list is made) Which idea sounds best to you?

G: Number 2. Want to act it out? I'll be her and you be me, OK?

P: (After a few practice rounds) Now you're ready to try it on your own, and if you want to talk some more, I'll be right here.

G: Thanks, Mom.

1. ignore her
2. Stand up to her
3. tell on her
4. do Something mean back to her
5. move to Peru

friends being cruel
to others

When girls you know are being cruel to others, it's hard to know what to do. Often you're just glad you're not the target. As long as you're not doing anything mean, you're not responsible, right?

Not exactly.

By standing by and doing nothing, you **ARE** doing something. You're letting the bully—and her victim—believe that you think what's happening between them is OK (when you know it's not).

When you see people being cruel, **don't ignore it.** Use body language that tells your friend you disapprove of what she's doing. Or say something—confront her, even if you know she may turn on you, too.

Do what seems right, but do something. It's called being a **good bystander,** and it can make a big difference. Besides, when you stand up for what you believe in, you'll be able to add "courageous" to the list of things that make you a great friend.

When have you stood up for something you believed in?

could you be a bully?

Ten ways to know

Do you need to be in charge all the time—
and hate it when you're not?

yes   no

Does a day hardly ever go by when you don't criticize somebody?

yes   no

Do you get mad at others when they don't do as you say?

yes   no

Do you make social "rules" that you expect others
to follow—and make threats when they don't?

yes   no

Are people afraid of how you're going to react?

yes   no

Have you made insulting remarks to people for things you
know they can't do anything about?

yes   no

Do you feel people should work to win your approval?

yes   no

Do you think it's OK to say mean things to people online?

yes   no

Do you decide who's in and who's out of your group?

yes   no

If you answered **yes** to any of these,

it's not OK.

Stop now. Try to figure out what's going on inside you. What makes you want to hurt other people? Have you been hurt? Are you angry? There are better ways to deal with your problems. Talk to someone who can help you sort out your feelings. The guidance office at school is often a good place to find help.

Control yourself, not your classmates. Truly, you'll be much happier —and so will those around you.

all about you

Think about the different groups at your school.

Are you in the "popular" group? Is this a good fit for you?
If it is, that's fine.

If you're not in the popular group, that's fine, too. If you like your
friends, if you make one another happy, then you're in the right place.

Big important point: Your happiness matters! It's basic: If the group you're in doesn't make you happy, what are you doing there? Never trade away happiness to fit in.

how much are you swayed by the crowd?

Rate yourself from **1** to **3.**

1 = I'd never do this.

2 = I might do this.

3 = I'd definitely do this.

_____ You talk less in the classes you have with the popular kids.

_____ You hate peppermints. "Want a peppermint?" asks Sabrina. You take it. Everyone else did.

_____ Here comes Dad, ready to take you to the school carnival —in an orange shirt! "You're NOT wearing that, are you?" you shriek.

_____ Allison, the most popular girl in school, has decided that Audrey is "out." You call Audrey and cancel the overnight you were planning for this weekend. You don't want to be "out," too.

_____ You had planned to go to a movie with your mom, but once you heard that "everyone" was going to the basketball game, you had to go, too. (You don't like basketball.)

_____ When you go shopping, you look for the exact style of shirt that you've seen the popular girls wear—even though you really like something else.

_____ Your friends say Community Leaders Club isn't cool. Even though you love it, you drop it.

answer:

If you answered **mostly 1s,** you make your own decisions, and that's good.

If you answered **mostly 2s,** you listen to your inner voice—when you aren't listening to the chorus. You could do better.

If you answered **mostly 3s,** you go whichever way the wind's blowing. Time to ask yourself a big question:

Who's in charge here, anyway?

Assuming Martians didn't remove your brain while no one was watching, the answer is—you.

Yes, life can be confusing, and **yes,** there are lots of decisions being thrown at you every day—but **don't** hand over to another girl the power to decide what's right for you. And **don't** choose friends who expect to have power over you. You want friends who like you as you are—truly as you are.

Friendship File

Janie

Janie and Cristeen had known each other since preschool. Janie was thoughtful and quiet. Cristeen loved the spotlight. They got along just fine until, as Janie put it, "Cristeen became a fashion freak from another world."

What happened

It all started over lip gloss. Yes, lip gloss. Cristeen loved wearing it and had every flavor in the universe clipped to her backpack. For Janie, on the other hand, lip gloss just wasn't her thing. She didn't want to wear it. Cristeen thought she should. That's when Cristeen and her group of friends started to hassle Janie about the clothes she wore. "Don't you own a pair of capri pants?" Cristeen would say. Janie didn't and didn't particularly want to. She liked her style. She did not like being teased.

What she did

Janie begged her mom for new clothes, even though she and her mom knew that wasn't the answer. Janie's mom suggested to Janie that she think about what she truly needed. Janie did, and the answer was better friends. She decided to work hard on developing a few really good friendships. She started with Natalie, a girl who had stuck up for her in the past. Janie called and thanked her. Their friendship blossomed from there. Then Cristeen started to give Natalie a hard time about hanging out with Janie. That was too much for Janie. She looked Cristeen in the eye and said, "You can't pick people's friends. If you don't like me, that's fine. You stay out of my way, and I'll stay out of yours." Janie had to say it only once. Everything changed.

How it worked out

Janie hung around with Natalie a lot. When Natalie hung out with Cristeen's group, Janie did, too. Yet Janie never fit in again, and she didn't try. If it was a good day, and the girls were playing something fun, she'd join in. But if they were looking over the latest fashion magazines and acting all goo-goo, Janie would steer clear. She didn't get invited to all the parties, but she didn't expect to. She was invited to some and went. By the end of the year, she had several girls to hang out with whom she really liked and who really liked her. Janie found that, for her, the goal was NOT to be popular. The goal was to be herself.

feeling good about yourself

You want to be **CONFIDENT** about who you are and what you believe in. When you're confident, you feel safe and in control of your life. Confidence helps you withstand rejection, even betrayal, because you know that it doesn't matter what the rule setters think about you. **What matters is what you think about yourself.**

How do you get to be confident?

Listen to the wise girl inside you. Don't stay with lousy friends just because you don't want to be alone. Being alone now and then in life is good. It helps you understand yourself in a new way and brings a special kind of contentment. And when you're happier with yourself, you've set the stage for really good friendships.

Think of a plant. Give it sunshine, water, good soil, and room to grow, and it will flourish, right? People are the same way. That wise girl inside needs attention, patience, and care, too. You need to nourish yourself with things that interest you, with the love of your family, and with hopes and dreams for the future.

When your self-esteem gets knocked around, you may need to do a little repair work, the same way you'd gather up a plant and put it back in the soil if it got knocked off the shelf.

quick fixes

Some days, you have the confidence to move mountains. Other days, you may need a boost. When that happens, try these ideas:

Make a list of **things you need to get done,** and then start tackling it. You'll feel great when you can check off each accomplishment.

Get creative! Use art, music, or poetry to express your feelings and lift your spirits.

Sometimes you can get so used to saying negative things about yourself that you start to believe them. Turn the self-doubt around by **finding positive messages to say to yourself.** When you hear the old messages start to creep in, stop, rewind, and start over!

Take a walk or a run—get up, get out, and move your body. **Exercise** can give you the energy you need to feel better.

List the **top ten reasons** that you wouldn't want to be anyone else but you.

Personalize your space. Make your room a reflection of you. Put up pictures of things that make you happy and express your spirit. Make signs that inspire you to feel good about yourself. Do the same thing to your locker.

Think of a person you really admire. Write down why. How can you be more like this person? Try to adopt some of the traits that you admire in other people.

Take a nap. The world looks a lot worse when you're exhausted from lack of sleep.

not-so-quick fixes

When a quick fix isn't enough, you may need to look at making some bigger changes in your life. Think of these activities as being like bridges, with a more confident you waiting on the other side.

Find new friends

Don't limit your friendships to kids at school. Look around. Is there someone in your life you would like to get to know better? It could be anyone. Think about the old woman down the street, kids from other schools, your softball coach, pen pals, the girl you take art lessons with, your aunt in Denver, or your cousin in Kalamazoo. Whoever it is, get in touch, reach out, and share some special time. It'll make your world bigger.

Take a stand

What do you stand for? On a piece of paper, make a list of some things that you feel strongly about, including the things you would—and wouldn't—do in the name of friendship. Keep it in your room and add to it often. If you know what you stand for, you'll have an easier time choosing friends who are right for you.

Find something that makes YOU happy

Deep inside everybody lies an intense interest in **SOMETHING.** Call it your passion. No, it's not about having a crush on a boy singer. This is an **inner passion**—something that brings you joy and confidence. When you have friendship troubles (or troubles of any other kind), your passion is a great place to turn. It doesn't really matter what your passion is. It could be playing tennis or the tuba. It could be reading or writing or drawing. It could be helping at the animal shelter. You decide. Just find something you love to do, and do it.

friends forever?

Having good friends requires that you be a good friend to yourself. You'll be happier, more confident, and more fun. You'll know good friendships from bad ones. And you'll take care of those good friendships by keeping communication open, admitting your mistakes, and expressing your feelings.

As you grow and change, your relationships will, too. Not all of your friendships are going to last forever. Some may not last long at all. But a girl who knows her own heart and mind has all she needs to choose and enjoy good friends . . . forever.

Have you had friendship troubles?
How did you work them out?
Send your true stories to:

Friendship Troubles Editor
American Girl
8400 Fairway Place
Middleton, WI 53562

Here are some other American Girl books you might like:

Each sold separately. Find more books online at americangirl.com.

Parents, request a FREE catalog at **americangirl.com/catalog.**
Sign up at **americangirl.com/email** to receive the latest news and exclusive offers

Discover online games, quizzes, activities,
and more at **americangirl.com**